Writing for *Challenger 2*

Skill-building writing exercises for each lesson in *Challenger 2*
of the *Challenger Adult Reading Series*

McVey & Associates, Inc.

NEW READERS PRESS

ISBN 1-56420-011-6

Copyright © 1994
New Readers Press
Publishing Division of ProLiteracy Worldwide
1320 Jamesville Avenue, Syracuse, New York 13210

Printed in the United States of America

20 19 18 17 16 15 14 13 12 11 10

Contents

Challenger 2

Challenger 2
Lesson 1 _____

1 **Choose the Right Word.** Read each sentence. From each pair of words, choose the right word to complete the sentence. Write the word in the blank.

child/children   1. Mrs. Clark had four _____.

draw/raw   2. I like to _____ with pen and ink.

touch/much   3. Ben won't _____ the wood saw.

cover/over   4. Mary paid _____ seven dollars for lunch.

mouth/month   5. The coffee was so hot, it burned June's _____.

sense/cents   6. Tom had enough _____ to know when to stop.

2 **Personal Questions.** Write sentences that answer the questions. Use words that tell about you.

1. What do you say when somebody sneezes? _____

_____

2. What do you do when you sneeze? _____

_____

3. What things make you sneeze? _____

_____

4. When do you sneeze the most? _____

_____

3 Unscramble the Sentences. Write sentences using the words below. Begin the first word of each sentence with a capital letter. Finish each sentence with a period.

1. Clark   worst   had   the   June   sneezing   fit

_____

2. noses   sneeze   cover   when   people   their   most   they

_____

4 Combine the Sentences. Combine each pair of sentences below to make one sentence.

1. Somebody may hear you sneezing. The person may say, "God bless you."

_____

2. June Clark had the worst sneezing fit ever recorded. She was seventeen years old at the time.

_____

_____

5 What Do You Think? Complete the sentences with words that tell what you think.

1. Sneezing can be a problem when _____

_____

2. If I had a sneezing fit, I would _____

_____

Challenger 2
Lesson 2 _____

1 Choose the Right Word. Read each sentence. From each pair of
words, choose the right word to complete the sentence. Write the word
in the blank.

catbird/catcall   1. A _____ is a shrill noise.

purring/barking   2. Dogs are often heard _____.

paws/arms   3. Cats and dogs both have _____.

cats/dogs   4. People say that _____ have nine lives.

2 Unscramble the Sentences. Write sentences using the words below.
Begin the first word of each sentence with a capital letter. Finish each
sentence with a period.

1. have cats own to their like way

_____

2. sharp cats smell of senses have and hearing

_____

3 What Do You Think? Complete the sentences with words that tell
what you think.

1. Many people have cats because _____

_____

2. The pet I would like to have is _____

_____

4 Combine the Sentences. Combine each pair of sentences below to make one sentence.

1. Dogs make good pets. Cats make good pets, too.

    _____

2. A doctor lived on the West Coast. He died in 1963.

    _____

3. The doctor had a will. The doctor left his money to his two cats.

    _____

5 Personal Questions. Write sentences that answer the questions. Use words that tell what you think.

1. What animals other than cats do people have as pets? _____

    _____

    _____

2. Which animal do you think is the smartest? _____

    _____

3. Why do you think people leave money to animals? _____

    _____

4. Besides leaving money to pets, what other strange things do animal lovers do?

    _____

    _____

Challenger 2
Lesson 3 _____

1 **Choose the Right Word.** Read each sentence. From each pair of
words, choose the right word to complete the sentence. Write the word
in the blank.

seven/ten   1. There are _____ cents in a dime.

hundred/five   2. A dollar has one _____ cents.

ninety/eighty   3. Seventy cents plus ten cents makes _____ cents.

hundred/thousand 4. There are one _____ cents in ten dollars.

2 **Unscramble the Sentences.** Write sentences using the words below.
Begin the first word of each sentence with a capital letter. Finish each
sentence with a period.

1. is people number for seven many a lucky

_____

2. body in years renewed human every the seven cells are

_____

3 **What Do You Think?** Complete the sentences with words that tell
what you think.

1. I think luck is _____

_____

2. Some people think bad luck comes from _____

_____

4 Combine the Sentences. Combine each pair of sentences below to make one sentence.

1. One woman quit smoking. She saved $1,500 in seven years.

   _____

   _____

2. There are seven days in a week. There are seven deadly sins.

   _____

   _____

3. A person who is missing for seven years is recorded as dead. This is the law.

   _____

   _____

5 Personal Questions. Write sentences that answer the questions. Use words that tell what you think.

1. Do you think someone who breaks a mirror will have bad luck? _____

   _____

   _____

2. Why do you think a person missing for seven years is recorded as dead? _____

   _____

   _____

3. Besides saving money, what else is good about not smoking? _____

   _____

   _____

Challenger 2
Lesson 4 _____

1 Choose the Right Word. Read each sentence. From each pair of words, choose the right word to complete the sentence. Write the word in the blank.

drink/drank   1. Joan doesn't _____ beer.

pints/quarts   2. A gallon has four _____.

pounds/pints   3. There are two _____ in a quart.

pubs/tubs   4. In England, bars are called _____.

England/English   5. People in many countries speak _____.

react/reach   6. If I eat too many berries, I _____ to them.

2 Combine the Sentences. Combine each pair of sentences below to make one sentence.

1. You can tell time in hours. You can tell time in seconds, too.

   _____

2. The word *cute* has an opposite. The opposite word is *ugly*.

   _____

3. Eddie always walks home from work. He always goes the same way.

   _____

4. The United States is big. The world is bigger.

   _____

10

3 What Do You Think? Complete the sentences with words that tell what you think.

1. People on the *Mayflower* drank beer because _____

    _____

2. If I were on a ship, I would like to eat _____

    _____

4 Unscramble the Sentences. Write sentences using the words below. Begin the first word of each sentence with a capital letter. Finish each sentence with a period.

1. would on *Mayflower* the gone the have south people further

    _____

2. smell it turns cloudy funny sunlight and a beer gives

    _____

5 Personal Questions. Write sentences that answer the questions. Use words that tell about you.

1. What foods would you take on a trip to a new land? _____

    _____

    _____

2. Do you think drinking beer is good or bad? _____

    _____

    _____

Challenger 2
Lesson 5 _____

1 **Choose the Right Word.** Read each sentence. From each pair of words, choose the right word to complete the sentence. Write the word in the blank.

paper/pepper   1. The salt and _____ are on the table.

chain/chair   2. John wore a gold _____ around his neck.

wrote/written   3. The scribe _____ the letter for the painter.

person/reason   4. It is important for you to meet that _____.

letters/vowels   5. There are twenty-six _____ in the alphabet.

2 **Unscramble the Sentences.** Write sentences using the words below. Begin the first word of each sentence with a capital letter. Finish each sentence with a period.

1. write   the   himself   the   lover   letter   not   did

_____

2. write   scribe   the   letter   to   hired   lover   the   a

_____

3. over   were   the   over   and   words   written

_____

4. job   this   boring   been   must   a   have

_____

3 What Do You Think? Complete the sentences with words that tell what you think.

1. A love letter should _____

_____

2. The scribe must have felt _____

_____

4 Combine the Sentences. Combine each pair of sentences below to make one sentence.

1. A scribe is a person. A scribe writes for a living.

_____

2. The lover stayed there. The lover said "I love you" 1,875,000 times.

_____

_____

5 Personal Questions. Write sentences that answer the questions. Use words that tell about you.

1. How would you tell someone about your feelings? _____

_____

_____

2. What is the most boring job you can think of? _____

_____

_____

Challenger 2
Lesson 6 _____

1 **Use These Words in Sentences.** Use some of the words below to write three sentences that tell something about the reading "Wigs."

bee's   bigwig   Egypt   England   floated   free
lice   shapes   shaved   wax   wigs   wool

1. _____

_____

2. _____

_____

3. _____

_____

2 **Personal Questions.** Write sentences that answer the questions. Use words that tell about you.

1. What do you do to make your hair look better? _____

_____

_____

2. Why might you wear a wig? _____

_____

_____

3. What kind of person would you call a "bigwig" today? _____

_____

_____

3 **Combine the Sentences.** Combine each pair of sentences below to make one sentence.

1.   Anne had a checkbook. The checkbook was easy to use.

   _____

2.   John had a girlfriend. His girlfriend's name was Linda.

   _____

3.   Shortstop is difficult to play. Shortstop is a position in baseball.

   _____

4.   Dan said, "Please give me some gingerbread." Dan also asked for milk.

   _____

4 **What Do You Think?** Complete the sentences with words that tell what you think.

1.   My hair "stands on end" when _____

   _____

   _____

2.   I "let my hair down" when _____

   _____

   _____

3.   A person who "gets in my hair" is _____

   _____

Challenger 2
Lesson 7 _____

1 **Unscramble the Sentences.** Write sentences using the words below. Begin the first word of each sentence with a capital letter. Finish each sentence with a period.

1. hidden   there   skunk's   a   are   pouches   under   tail

   _____

2. six   enough   each   liquid   has   rounds   pouch   for

   _____

3. week   more   takes   to   liquid   form   a   it

   _____

2 **Combine the Sentences.** Combine each pair of sentences below to make one sentence.

1. That problem looked hard. It was really easy to do.

   _____

   _____

2. Sometimes I forget important things. I remember them later.

   _____

   _____

3. Mary saved money buying a used car. She still spent a lot of money.

   _____

   _____

3 **Use These Words in Sentences.** Use some of the words below to write three sentences that tell something about the reading "Skunks."

     chased   forefeet   liquid   pouches   range

     shoots   six-shooter   skunk   straight   trouble

1. _____

   _____

2. _____

   _____

3. _____

   _____

4 **Personal Questions.** Write sentences that answer the questions. Use words that tell what you think.

1. What would you do if you came face-to-face with a skunk? _____

   _____

   _____

2. How do you act when you think you are in danger? _____

   _____

   _____

3. How do some other people act when they think they are in danger? _____

   _____

   _____

Challenger 2
Lesson 8 _____

1 **Choose the Right Word.** Read each sentence. From each pair of
words, choose the right word to complete the sentence. Write the word
in the blank.

hatch/watch   1. The eggs _____ during one week.

shell/spell   2. The chick pecks against the _____.

peeping/peeking   3. The new chick makes _____ sounds.

chicken/children 4. Which came first, the _____ or the egg?

clutch/touch   5. A group of eggs laid at one time is called a _____.

2 **What Do You Think?** Complete the sentences with words that tell
what you think.

1. "Counting one's chickens before they hatch" means _____

   _____

   _____

2. It is not smart to "put all your eggs in one basket" because _____

   _____

   _____

3. If you try to do something and "lay an egg," you _____

   _____

   _____

3 Put These Sentences in Order. Write these sentences in the correct time order on the lines below.

Air gets into the eggs.

Eggs are laid at one time.

The eggs hatch within a few hours of each other.

The sounds are heard by the other chicks.

The chicks peck against the shells.

1. _____

2. _____

3. _____

4. _____

5. _____

4 Personal Questions. Write sentences that answer the questions. Use words that tell what you think.

1. Do you think animals talk to each other? _____

   _____

   _____

2. Besides talking, how else do humans share ideas with each other? _____

   _____

   _____

3. What are some problems people can have because they don't share ideas? _____

   _____

   _____

Challenger 2
Lesson 9 _____

1 **Combine the Sentences.** Combine each pair of sentences below to make one sentence.

1. John A. Sutter owned land. Gold was found on Sutter's land.

   _____

2. The real gold rush began in 1849. That year 100,000 men rushed to California.

   _____

2 **Unscramble the Sentences.** Write sentences using the words below. Begin the first word of each sentence with a capital letter. Finish each sentence with a period.

1. was   his   gold   as   word   good   as

   _____

2. in   was   thought   land   El Dorado   there   rich   a   people   called   gold

   _____

3 **What Do You Think?** Complete the sentences with words that tell what you think.

1. People looked for El Dorado because _____

   _____

2. If there were a gold rush today, I think my friends would _____

   _____

4 **Use These Words in Sentences.** Use some of the words below to write three sentences that tell something about the reading "Gold."

California   dollars   forty-niners   gold   lonely

miners   news   ounce   pan   shacks   Sutter

1. _____

_____

2. _____

_____

3. _____

_____

5 **Personal Questions.** Write sentences that answer the questions. Use words that tell about you.

1. Would you take a job far from your home to make more money? _____

_____

_____

2. How might your family feel if you took a job far from your home?_____

_____

_____

3. How would you deal with being lonely if you worked far from your home? _____

_____

_____

Challenger 2
Lesson 10 _____

1 **Choose the Right Word.** Read each sentence. From each pair of
words, choose the right word to complete the sentence. Write the
word in the blank.

though/through   1. Are you _____ with your dinner?

spot/sport   2. The _____ John likes best is baseball.

stick/stuck   3. The car was _____ in the ditch for an hour.

rhyme/crime   4. *June, tune,* and *moon* all _____ with *spoon.*

2 **Unscramble the Sentences.** Write sentences using the words below.
Begin the first word of each sentence with a capital letter. Finish each
sentence with a period.

1. rhymes   been   Goose   for   of   years   Mother   around   have   hundreds

   _____

2. of   loved   tease   one   to   lords   queen   her   England

   _____

3 **What Do You Think?** Complete the sentences with words that tell
what you think.

1. People make up rhymes about others because _____

   _____

2. Nicknames may be used in rhymes because _____

   _____

3. The queen of England had someone taste her soup because _____

_____

4 **Put These Sentences in Order.** Write these sentences in the correct time order on the lines below.

> The "Dish" and the "Spoon" ran off to get married.
>
> The people who served the queen had nicknames.
>
> A lady-in-waiting was called "Spoon."
>
> Somebody made up a rhyme about the "Dish" and the "Spoon."

1. _____

2. _____

3. _____

4. _____

_____

5 **Personal Questions.** Write sentences that answer the questions. Use words that tell about you.

1. Who do you know who likes to make up rhymes? _____

_____

_____

2. What special nicknames do you or your friends have? _____

_____

_____

3. What nickname might you give someone who likes to dance and sing?_____

_____

_____

Challenger 2
Lesson 11 _____

1 Use These Words in Sentences. Use some of the words below to write three sentences that tell something about the reading "Sleeping."

body   brain   breathing   heart   limp   relaxes

REM sleep   stages   turning   yawning

1. _____

_____

2. _____

_____

3. _____

_____

2 Combine the Sentences. Combine each pair of sentences below to make one sentence.

1. Most dreaming takes place during the fourth stage of sleep. The fourth stage is called REM.

_____

_____

2. REM is the deepest sleep. During REM, the body is very limp.

_____

_____

3. We need to move during the time we sleep. This is so we will not get sick.

_____

_____

3 **What Do You Think?** Complete the answers to the questions with words that tell what you think.

1. Do you think the changes in your body during sleep are good for you?

   I think the changes during sleep _____

   _____

2. What might happen to our bodies if we did not sleep?

   If we did not sleep, our bodies _____

   _____

3. Do you think dreaming is important?

   I think dreaming is (isn't) important because _____

   _____

4 **Complete These Paragraphs.** Complete the following paragraphs in your own words.

1. Sometimes I yawn when I am sleepy. When I yawn a lot, I know _____

   _____

2. People move twenty to forty-five times every night. I know I move when I sleep

   because _____

   _____

3. I sometimes have dreams when I sleep. When I wake up, I _____

   _____

   _____

Challenger 2

Lesson 12 _____

1 **Choose the Right Word.** Choose the correctly spelled word from each
pair of words to complete the sentence. Write the correctly spelled
word in the blank.

suny/sunny   1. What a _____ day this is!

noisey/noisy   2. The honeybees were very _____.

snapy/snappy   3. John was wearing a _____ red hat.

wavy/wavey   4. The lake was very _____ during the storm.

budy/buddy   5. My son's best _____ stayed overnight with him.

2 **What Do You Think?** Complete the answers to the questions with
words that tell what you think.

1. Why do you think people like to eat honey?

   I think people like to eat honey because _____

   _____

2. In what ways are worker bees like humans?

   Worker bees are like humans _____

   _____

3. Why is the sense of smell important to a honeybee?

   The sense of smell is important to a honeybee because _____

   _____

26

3 Put These Sentences in Order. Write these sentences in the correct time order on the lines below.

The drones starve to death.

The queen lays her eggs.

In the fall, the honey flow is over.

The drones mate with a young queen.

1. _____

2. _____

3. _____

4. _____

4 Complete These Paragraphs. Complete the following paragraphs in your own words.

1. Some worker bees stand guard at the hive. Other workers _____

   _____

   _____

2. People are sometimes called "drones" when they don't work very hard. People make me

   think of drones when they _____

   _____

3. Sometimes people, like bees, don't have enough food to feed a large group. But people

   have ways to get more food. People can _____

   _____

   _____

Challenger 2
Lesson 13 _____

1 **Use These Words in Sentences.** Use some of the words below to write three sentences that tell something about the reading "Handwriting."

     cases   expert   factor   handwriting   letters

     line   police   slant   wide   writer

1. _____

_____

2. _____

_____

3. _____

_____

2 **What Do You Think?** Complete the answers to the questions with words that tell what you think.

1. Do you think your handwriting tells people about you?

I think my handwriting _____

_____

_____

2. Why do you think the police call upon handwriting experts for help?

I think the police call upon handwriting experts _____

_____

_____

3 **Unscramble the Sentences.** Write sentences using the words below. Begin the first word of each sentence with a capital letter. Finish each sentence with a period.

1. many look experts factors handwriting at

   _____

2. about slant the of writer the letters the tells

   _____

4 **Combine the Sentences.** Combine each pair of sentences below to make one sentence.

1. That bill is due tomorrow. I paid it yesterday.

   _____

2. The young woman won the race. The older woman did very well in the race also.

   _____

5 **Complete These Paragraphs.** Complete the following paragraphs in your own words.

1. Handwriting experts say they can tell a lot about people. I think handwriting experts

   _____

   _____

2. An expert knows things other people don't know. People can become experts by

   _____

   _____

Challenger 2
Lesson 14 _____

1 **Choose the Right Word.** Read each sentence. From each pair of
words, choose the right word to complete the sentence. Write the word
in the blank.

keep/kept   1. The phone _____ ringing all day long.

diver/river   2. Jill is the best _____ on the swim team.

won't/wouldn't   3. Dad said, "I _____ do that if I were you."

nowhere/   4. The missing notebook was _____ to be found.
anywhere

flood/food   5. Most of Linda's household goods were lost in the

                      _____ .

2 **What Do You Think?** Complete the answers to the questions with
words that tell what you think.

1. What do you think were the worst things about being a slave?

   I think the worst things about being a slave were _____

   _____

2. What do you think were the worst things about being set free?

   I think the worst things about being set free were_____

   _____

3. What do you think were the best things about being set free?

   I think the best things about being set free were _____

   _____

3 **Put These Sentences in Order.** Write these sentences in the correct time order on the lines below.

> An ex-slave wrote a story about her life.
>
> The slaves were set free in 1863.
>
> The War Between the States started.
>
> The slaves dreamed about freedom.

1. _____

2. _____

3. _____

4. _____

4 **Complete These Paragraphs.** Complete the following paragraphs in your own words.

1. The slaves had always wanted to be free. When they got their freedom, it wasn't like

   they hoped it would be because _____

   _____

   _____

2. Sometimes we hope and pray for things for a long time. But when we get those things,

   they don't seem to be what we wanted. Instead, _____

   _____

   _____

3. Sometimes I dream of doing something new. Before I try the new thing, I _____

   _____

   _____

Challenger 2
Lesson 15 _____

1 **Use These Words in Sentences.** Use some of the words below to write three sentences that tell something about the reading "A Very Strange Hobby."

barbed   helicopter   hobby   hooked   rare

snag   spare   strand   swizzle   wire

1. _____

   _____

2. _____

   _____

3. _____

   _____

2 **What Do You Think?** Complete the answers to the questions with words that tell what you think.

1. What kinds of things help us learn about the past?

   We can learn about the past from _____

   _____

   _____

2. What kinds of hobbies do you think are good to have?

   I think good hobbies are _____

   _____

   _____

3 Unscramble the Sentences. Write sentences using the words below. Begin the first word of each sentence with a capital letter. Finish each sentence with a period.

1. of wire of a name is Hold Fast barbed the kind

   _____

2. to store wire barbed sticks were a sold swizzle

   _____

3. kinds around wire no some are barbed of longer

   _____

4 Combine the Sentences. Combine each pair of sentences below to make one sentence.

1. The doctor has wire cutters. He uses them to cut off a strand of wire.

   _____

2. Some barbed wire is rare. Rare barbed wire may sell for forty dollars a strand.

   _____

5 Complete These Paragraphs. Complete the following paragraphs in your own words.

1. People have many hobbies. Some people trade baseball cards. Others _____

   _____

2. A hobby is something people do in their spare time. Other things people do in their

   spare time are _____

   _____

Challenger 2

Lesson 16 _____

1 **Choose the Right Word.** Read each sentence. From each pair of
words, choose the right word to complete the sentence. Write the word
in the blank.

bang/bank   1. The _____ closes early today.

which/witch   2. Jack did not know _____ bus to take.

dam/damp   3. The clothes on the line were still _____.

sweat/sweater   4. The room was hot, so I took off my _____.

loss/lost   5. I _____ my new hat the day after Christmas.

2 **What Do You Think?** Answer the questions with words that tell what
you think.

1. Whales are in danger of being killed off. What can be done to help whales? _____

   _____

   _____

2. What other animals do you think are in danger of being killed off? _____

   _____

   _____

3. What do you think will happen if we kill off many kinds of animals? _____

   _____

   _____

3 Put These Sentences in Order. Write these sentences in the correct time order on the lines below.

        Whales became shaped like fish.

        Whales used to walk on land.

        Whales are hunted and are being killed off.

        Whales left the land to live in the water.

1. _____

2. _____

3. _____

4. _____

4 Complete These Paragraphs. Complete the following paragraphs in your own words.

1. Whales and fish are alike in many ways. Both whales and fish _____

_____

_____

2. In other ways, fish and whales are not alike. Fish breathe _____

_____

_____

3. Fish and whales do not give birth in the same ways. Fish _____

_____

_____

Challenger 2
Lesson 17 _____

1 **Use These Words in Sentences.** Use some of the words and phrases below to write three sentences that tell something about the reading "Black Bart."

    box   Charles   hold up   joke   plans
    riding shotgun   robbed   scare   stagecoaches   teacher

1. _____

_____

2. _____

_____

3. _____

_____

2 **What Do You Think?** Answer the questions with words that tell what you think.

1. What are some dangers Black Bart faced as a robber that he did not face as a

teacher? _____

_____

_____

2. How might Black Bart have been caught after eight years? _____

_____

_____

3 **Unscramble the Sentences.** Write sentences using the words below. Begin the first word of each sentence with a capital letter. Finish each sentence with a period.

1. was Charles first Black Bart's name real

   _____

2. to stick as broke a a from he bush a gun use

   _____

4 **Combine the Sentences.** Combine each pair of sentences below to make one sentence.

1. He always laid careful plans. He always kept his plans to himself.

   _____

2. He knew the driver. He thought he'd give him a scare.

   _____

5 **Complete These Paragraphs.** Complete the following paragraphs in your own words.

1. There are many reasons against robbing people. One reason is that _____

   _____

   _____

2. People sometimes admire men like Black Bart. I think _____

   _____

   _____

Challenger 2
Lesson 18 _____

1 **Choose the Right Word.** Read each sentence. From each pair of
words, choose the right word to complete the sentence. Write the word
in the blank.

million/billion   1. Many people think the earth is more than two

_____ years old.

slowly/quickly   2. The hot, whirling gases _____ cooled.

gas/solid   3. The earth's shell changed from a liquid to a _____.

sinks/basins   4. Rains filled the ocean _____.

2 **What Do You Think?** Answer the questions with words that tell what
you think.

1. The reading tells one idea about how the earth was formed. What other ideas do some

   people have about how the earth was formed? _____

   _____

   _____

2. How do you think the earth was formed? _____

   _____

   _____

3. Do you think we will ever know for sure how the earth was formed? Why or why not?

   _____

   _____

3 **Unscramble the Sentences.** Write sentences using the words below. Begin the first word of each sentence with a capital letter. Finish each sentence with a period.

1. gases into the and liquid flaming turned cooled

   _____

2. state the shell a solid earth's changed outer to

   _____

3. fell hundreds the for of rains years

   _____

4. forms life oceans simple of in one-celled began the

   _____

5. was land on there for years of no the millions life

   _____

4 **Complete This Paragraph.** Complete the following paragraph in your own words.

   The earth must have been a strange place when there were no plants, no animals, and

no human beings. I think the earth may have looked like _____

_____

_____

_____

_____

Challenger 2
Lesson 19 _____

1 **Use These Words in Sentences.** Use some of the words below to
write three sentences that tell something about the reading "Jails on
the High Seas."

    awful   convicts   fastest   galley   lice

    oar   port   screams   washed   whips

1. _____

   _____

2. _____

   _____

3. _____

   _____

2 **Combine the Sentences.** Combine each pair of sentences below to
make one sentence.

1. The convicts would push the oar and dip it into the water. They would pull with all
their might.

   _____

   _____

2. A convict lived with the men in his gang. He did this until the end of his days.

   _____

   _____

3 Unscramble the Sentences. Write sentences using the words below. Begin the first word of each sentence with a capital letter. Finish each sentence with a period.

1. was convict a no galleys man a longer the on

   _____

2. sea galley hell on life board a living at was a

   _____

4 What Do You Think? Answer the questions with words that tell what you think.

1. What does the saying "You're only as old as you feel" mean? _____

   _____

   _____

2. What does it mean to say, "One picture is worth a thousand words"? _____

   _____

   _____

5 Complete This Paragraph. Complete the following paragraph in your own words.

   A long time ago, galleys were rowed by convicts chained to their oars. Not so long

ago, convicts in the United States were chained together and forced to build roads and

work on farms. I think using convicts to do these kinds of jobs is _____

   _____

   _____

   _____

Challenger 2
Lesson 20 _____

1 **Use These Words in Sentences.** Use some of the words below to write three sentences that tell something about the reading "The Father of Our Country."

birthday   bodyguard   English   first   kidnap

king   president   richest   swearing   terms

1. _____

_____

2. _____

_____

3. _____

_____

2 **What Do You Think?** Answer the questions with words that tell what you think.

1. Why do you think Washington told one person never to say he should be king? _____

_____

_____

2. Do you think it is better to have a king or a president? Why?_____

_____

_____

3. Do you think Washington was right to call swearing a "mean and low" vice? Why or

why not? _____

_____

3 Put These Sentences in Order. Write these sentences in the correct time order on the lines below.

His friends had to lend him money to go to New York.

George Washington was born on February 11.

He served two terms as president.

Men tried to kidnap Washington in order to kill him.

1. _____

2. _____

3. _____

4. _____

4 Complete These Paragraphs. Complete the following paragraphs in your own words.

1. We all know many common sayings. A common saying I use a lot is _____

   _____

   _____

   _____

   _____

2. Everyone likes to get a pat on the back now and then. A time when a pat on the back

   made me feel good was _____

   _____

   _____

   _____

   _____

Challenger 2
Review _____

1 **Unscramble the Sentences.** Write sentences using the words below.
Each sentence is a common saying. Begin the first word of each
sentence with a capital letter. Finish each sentence with a period.

1. ton hit of a it him bricks like

   _____

2. sleeve wear don't your heart your on

   _____

3. in put basket eggs don't all your one

   _____

4. count your don't hatched until are chickens they

   _____

2 **What Do You Think?** Answer the questions to tell what you think.

1. If you could buy anything you wanted, what would it be? Why? _____

   _____

   _____

2. If you could live anywhere you wanted, where would it be? Why? _____

   _____

   _____

3. If you could have any job you wanted, what would it be? Why? _____

   _____

   _____

3 Put These Sentences in Order. Write these sentences in the correct time order on the lines below.

        Mike gave his car keys to a friend who wasn't drinking.

        Mike drove two of his friends to a party.

        Mike's friend drove everyone home from the party.

        Mike drank a number of beers at the party.

1. _____

2. _____

3. _____

4. _____

4 Combine the Sentences. Combine each pair of sentences below to make one sentence.

1. Sixty people went to the dance. They all had a good time.

   _____

   _____

2. Teachers help people learn. People must learn things for themselves.

   _____

   _____

3. You can take care of yourself. Eating good food, getting enough sleep, and working out are things you can do.

   _____

   _____

5 **Complete These Paragraphs.** Complete the following paragraphs in your own words.

1. People can help themselves in many ways. They can take classes to learn new things. Many things people learn can save them money. People can save money if they learn to

   _____

   _____

   _____

   _____

2. People can make their homes nicer, too. They can make an apartment or a house nicer if they learn how to _____

   _____

   _____

3. People feel better if they eat right. They can help themselves eat right if they learn how to

   _____

   _____

   _____

4. I can take classes to learn things I don't know. Some of the things I would like to learn are

   _____

   _____

   _____